IDENTIFYING AND DOCUMENTING A COMMUNITY PROBLEM FOR A POLITICAL CAMPAIGN

Angie Timmons

New York

Published in 2020 by The Rosen Publishing Group, Inc.
29 East 21st Street, New York, NY 10010

Copyright © 2020 by The Rosen Publishing Group, Inc.

First Edition

All rights reserved. No part of this book may be reproduced in any form without permission in writing from the publisher, except by a reviewer.

Library of Congress Cataloging-in-Publication Data

Names: Timmons, Angie, author.
Title: Identifying and documenting a community problem for a political campaign / Angie Timmons.
Description: New York : Rosen Publishing, 2020 | Series: Be the change! : political participation in your community | Includes bibliographical references and index. | Audience: Grade 7 to 12.
Identifiers: LCCN 2019013273| ISBN 9781725340848 (library bound) | ISBN 9781725340831 (pbk.)
Subjects: LCSH: Political campaigns—Juvenile literature. | Political participation—Juvenile literature. | Community organization—Juvenile literature.
Classification: LCC JF2112.C3 T54 2019 | DDC 324.7—dc23
LC record available at https://lccn.loc.gov/2019013273

Manufactured in the United States of America

CONTENTS

INTRODUCTION **4**

CHAPTER ONE
IDENTIFYING THE PROBLEMS IN YOUR COMMUNITY **7**

CHAPTER TWO
UNDERSTANDING THE COMMUNITY **17**

CHAPTER THREE
ASSESSING A CANDIDATE **28**

CHAPTER FOUR
IT'S YOUR TURN **40**

GLOSSARY **51**
FOR MORE INFORMATION **53**
FOR FURTHER READING **56**
BIBLIOGRAPHY **57**
INDEX **61**

INTRODUCTION

On the afternoon of February 14, 2018, nineteen-year-old Nikolas Cruz paid a visit to his former high school, Marjory Stoneman Douglas High School in Parkland, Florida, armed with an AR-15 assault-style rifle. Cruz opened fire, killed fourteen students and three staff members, wounded fifteen other people, then snuck out of the school amidst the crowd of people fleeing for their lives. He was apprehended an hour later and eventually charged with seventeen counts of premeditated murder.

The Stoneman Douglas shooting was the worst high school shooting since the April 20, 1999, massacre at Columbine High School in Colorado, in which two twelfth graders killed twelve of their fellow students and one teacher before committing suicide in the school library. School shootings became an unfortunately common news headline in the years that followed Columbine. A February 14, 2018, *Washington Post* article reported that since 2000, more than 130 shootings had occurred at American elementary, middle, and high schools. More than fifty shootings had happened at colleges and universities.

Shortly after the shooting at Marjory Stoneman Douglas High School, a group of students who survived the shooting sprang into action. In the wake of the tragedy, they made use of the press attention to share

INTRODUCTION

The March for Our Lives movement, which was started by survivors of a high school shooting, called attention to the issue of gun violence and the need for reform.

their stories and call for gun reform measures. Inspired by the students' bravery, supporters across the nation demonstrated outside of state houses, flooded elected officials with phone calls and letters, and staged school walkouts to demand tighter gun control laws.

On March 24, just one month and ten days after the shooting, the Stoneman Douglas survivors brought their demands for gun control legislation to Washington, DC, by organizing a huge demonstration called the March for Our Lives. Hundreds of thousands of supporters held satellite marches in cities around the world.

What began as a group of high school students protesting against gun violence turned into the activist organization March for Our Lives. The organization has developed a comprehensive policy agenda and its members actively pressure lawmakers to draft and adopt gun control measures. The founders of March for Our Lives stayed active and loud throughout 2018 and urged voters to pressure their elected officials on the issue of gun control, making it a key issue in the run-up to the midterm elections. On November 6, 2018, Democrats—most of whom openly supported gun reform measures during their campaigns—became the majority party in the US House of Representatives.

March for Our Lives is a powerful example of what can happen when young people identify a problem, document their experiences, and demand that political candidates and elected officials acknowledge and address the problem. While the future of gun control legislation in the United States is unclear, the Stoneman Douglas survivors reminded the public that important things can be accomplished when people work toward solving community problems. They showed that power lies within the will of the people and that elected representatives should remember that they work on behalf of the people they represent.

CHAPTER ONE

IDENTIFYING THE PROBLEMS IN YOUR COMMUNITY

Communities take all forms: families, schools, faith-based organizations, towns, regions, states, ethnic groups, the list goes on. You are part of several communities, whether you realize it or not.

"The idea of having a 'community' at all might feel foreign to you, whether you're living in your hometown or you change addresses with the seasons," wrote Jackie Bernstein in Bustle. "But even if you feel like your community is just an accident of where you were born, or the place where you attend school or work, it can be much more than that."

Nations are comprised of millions of communities, each with its own identity, culture, concerns, and needs. Like individual people, each community has its own problems. But in any given town, county, congressional district, and state, these individual communities occasionally come together for one unified purpose: electing public officials.

Communities are made up of people who have something in common. This could be where you live, how you identify, or what you believe in. Every community has its own needs.

WHAT'S SO INTERESTING ABOUT ELECTIONS?

Political elections are a vital part of a democracy. If that statement makes you feel like yawning, think about why that is and what you can do to change it! What pops into your mind when you think of the word "politics"? Maybe you imagine boring government stuff that older people are supposed to deal with. Maybe you remember a scandal involving a politician. You may imagine a government building full of men and women you've never heard of, bickering over complicated issues. Considering some of these common

Identifying the Problems in Your Community

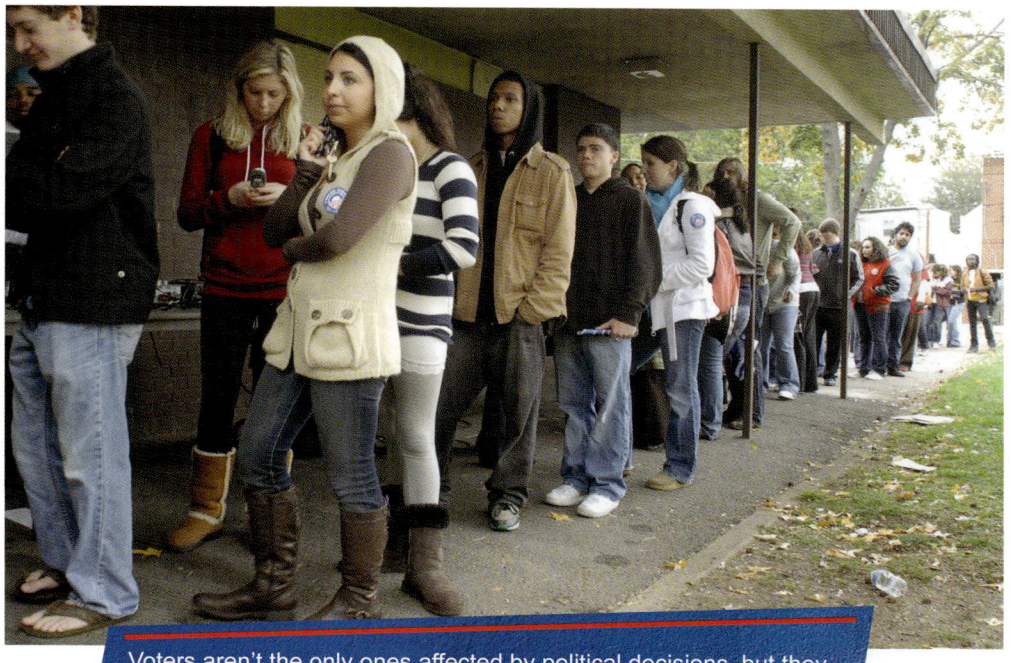
Voters aren't the only ones affected by political decisions, but they do choose who gets to make those decisions. That's why political participation is so important.

associations, you may wonder why politics gets so much attention.

Political elections get a lot of attention because their outcomes directly affect everyone. Elections give voters the chance to make choices that determine everything from who will make decisions about your education to who will lead the nation for the next four years. For many people, elections are the only time they get to make their voices heard on issues they care about, such as the environment, education, or health care. Even if you aren't yet old enough to vote, elections are a great way to learn about politicians, candidates, and problems or issues that impact you and your future.

DECISION MAKERS

The United States is a republic in which the power is held by the people and the representatives (sometimes called elected officials or lawmakers) elected by the people. The highest elected office in the land is president, but many different elected officials on local, state, and federal levels make decisions that impact people's lives.

Locally, most towns have an elected mayor and city council. These representatives vote on matters such as how much money city departments (like the police) get each year and on some taxation issues. Local school boards—either elected by voters or appointed by another authority, such as a mayor—make decisions related to education. Judges are often elected, and in some states, local sheriffs are elected.

On the state level, elected governors and elected legislatures meet in state capitals and work on laws specific to their state. Legislatures typically comprise senators and representatives who are elected by voters from their home districts.

Members of the US Congress (divided into the House of Representatives and the Senate) are elected by voters in their home states. Every state gets two senators, while the number of House representatives each state gets is based on the state's population.

Why does it matter who governs in your town, school district, or state? There are a few reasons. Most politics is local, meaning a lot of what happens in your life is decided on the local or state level. It also matters because local government is often a stepping-stone for people who aspire to higher elected offices. Many US senators, congresspeople, and presidents started in local or state government. The more good people are elected locally, the more good people are likely to be elected to higher levels of office in the future.

UNDERSTANDING CAMPAIGNS

Every year, some kind of election happens. Some of those elections are local, such as elections for mayor or school board, and some are special elections to fill an open seat on a local governing board or to vote on certain issues. Every two years, there are midterm elections, in which voters can elect state, local, and national representatives and other officeholders in the middle of the president's four-year term. Every four years, people vote for the president of the United States.

In the run-up to these elections, candidates run campaigns to try to win the support of their constituents. You may have seen people handing out campaign literature on the street or notice political signs posted in your neighbors' front yards. You may have even attended a political rally. These are all

Campaigns give candidates the opportunity to gain name recognition and share their political platforms before the election and to drum up support among voters.

examples of political campaigning, an often creative and intense process by which candidates for public office make their case to voters. Campaigns can go on for months or even years, depending on the office a candidate is running for. They can get very heated and personal, especially when the race between two candidates is close.

Political campaigns provide a way for candidates to communicate with their constituents about their positions on various issues. They help candidates get to know the people and the communities they hope to represent, and they allow those people and communities to get to know the candidates. Voters depend on campaigns to figure out what decisions they'll make at the voting booth on Election Day. Candidates depend on campaigns not only to persuade voters to support them, but also to set themselves apart from other people running for office. One way they set themselves apart is in how they address community problems during their campaigns and how they propose solving those problems.

POLITICS STARTS WITH YOU

Consider something you want or consider a priority, such getting accepted onto a team or being admitted to your college of choice. Now consider some problems you might be worried about: grades, a fight with a friend, a date, bullying, paying for college, or getting along with your parents.

How does it feel to think that you might not get the things you want? How does it feel to wonder if the problems you're worried about will ever be resolved?

Identifying the Problems in Your Community 13

WHAT IS A COMMUNITY PROBLEM?

There's a long list of issues that qualify as community problems. Some are obvious because they affect most communities and are easily recognizable. These are things like violence, homelessness, poverty, economic recession, or inadequate transportation. Other community problems and their impacts can be harder to detect. These things may include racial discrimination, drug addiction, lack of health care, domestic violence, child or animal abuse, economic inequality, and environmental damage.

Your specific communities, such as your school, may face other problems not listed here. Think critically about this. What problems do you see or hear about? What bothers you? What would you like to see fixed? To identify a community problem, consider:

- how frequently it occurs
- how long it's been going on
- how many people it affects
- how severe it is
- if it creates inequality or denies people certain rights
- how people in the community view the problem.

Once a community problem has been identified, the next step is figuring out how it became a problem.

Usually, problems are symptoms of something else. For example, Nikolas Cruz exhibited symptoms indicating that he was capable of violence before the Stoneman Douglas High School shooting. He was isolated and angry (symptoms) after the death of his mother and after multiple schools couldn't help resolve his developmental and emotional issues (problem). He posted about violence and killing (symptoms) but was able to buy guns anyway (problem). If Cruz's peers and community

(CONTINUED ON THE NEXT PAGE)

Identifying and Documenting a Community Problem for a Political Campaign

(CONTINUED FROM THE PREVIOUS PAGE)

members had intervened after identifying his symptoms and the associated problems, the tragic shooting might have been prevented.

The students who formed March for Our Lives recognized these symptoms and community problems, and they came together to take action. They showed that it's possible to make a huge difference in communities by documenting the problem, developing strategies to address it, and demanding lawmakers do something about it.

Is this a problem or the symptom of a problem? It's an important distinction to make when evaluating community issues, what causes them, and how they might be fixed.

Chances are, you feel frustrated because so much of your life is in the hands of other people, like your parents, teachers, college admissions boards, or even classmates. Wouldn't it be nice to have the chance to have more say in the decisions that impact you? Or to have the chance to find people who not only share your concerns, but also want to fix them?

Identifying the Problems in Your Community   15

In the world of politics, elections give voters the opportunity to vote for people they hope will positively impact their lives and solve problems they're worried about. Campaigns give people the opportunity to share their priorities and concerns with candidates and find out what those candidates plan to do about them. On the campaign trail, candidates will learn about communities and their problems. This provides a valuable education for candidates because most of politics involves handling community problems. In fact, most legislation is reactive, meaning lawmakers enact laws in response to problems, rather than making laws as a preventive measure for a problem that hasn't happened yet.

During a campaign, political candidates should do all they can to become acquainted with the various needs of the communities they hope to represent.

Many young people don't think politics matters because they don't see much connection between their own personal concerns and what the government does. Some disregard politics because they're not old enough to vote. Gareth Morgans, a Houston-based political campaign adviser who's worked on fifteen campaigns, gave the following advice in an interview with the author:

> You might not be able to vote now, but the people that are voting now are making decisions that will impact you in your future: whether it's your family, education and training, future job opportunities, and quality of life … While you might not be able to vote now, you can make sure your voice is heard by the people voting now, and heard by the people they elect.

CHAPTER TWO

UNDERSTANDING THE COMMUNITY

In 1985, Barack Obama had recently graduated from Columbia University and was having trouble finding a job when he applied to work for the Developing Communities Project (DCP), an organization formed in 1984 to help people affected by widespread unemployment in Chicago. DCP was operated by community organizers—people who bring together community members to work toward common goals and solutions.

DCP was trying to bring together Chicago's historically divided white and black communities to work on employment solutions that would benefit everyone. Organizers at DCP believed that Obama's background and experiences as the son of a white American mother and a Kenyan father could help him bring together different communities. What they didn't know when they hired Obama was that this community organizing position was laying the foundation for his future presidential campaign.

COMMUNITY ORGANIZING: THE BEST EDUCATION

Before working with DCP, Obama had never really been forced to consider the role that his race played in his interactions with the communities he identified with. Working for DCP, however, he spent a lot of time interacting with black communities for the first time. He showed an ability to interact with and be accepted by people from a diverse range of communities. He also had an uncanny ability to convince different communities to set aside their differences and work together. This was the beginning of Obama's political journey.

Obama believed that feeling a sense of community and belonging could help people take an interest in politics and inspire them to get involved. Instead of staging protests to demand more jobs and economic opportunities (the way things had been done in Chicago for a long time), Obama brought together community leaders to work on the city's problems. For example, in an unprecedented collaborative achievement, Obama got the leaders of nearly all of Chicago's religious groups to meet and identify and strategize about community problems and solutions. In turn, those religious leaders got members of their faith communities to get involved. This resulted in thousands of people of diverse faiths, races, ethnicities, backgrounds, and political affiliations working together to solve community problems.

After three years with DCP, Obama went on to earn a law degree at Harvard University, get elected to the

Understanding the Community

President Barack Obama's journey to the highest office in the land began on a community level. This experience helped him inspire many communities and voters during his presidential campaign.

Illinois State Senate, and eventually, get elected to the US Senate. He became the Democratic nominee for president in the 2008 election and won, becoming the first black president of the United States. He served two terms. Obama has described his three years of community organizing with DCP as the best education he ever received and one of the main reasons he was a successful presidential candidate.

INSPIRING COMMUNITIES

As a presidential candidate, Obama electrified diverse segments of the electorate. His campaign rallies were widely attended by people from diverse backgrounds.

He spoke sincerely about his personal background and his work as a community organizer, showing a direct understanding of common problems, such as unemployment and lack of health insurance. Obama encouraged the black community, a historically underrepresented political community, to participate in the democratic process: the number of black voters in the 2008 presidential election jumped almost 10 percent compared to the 2004 presidential race between Republican George W. Bush and Democrat John Kerry.

Obama also inspired young people to participate in the political process: about half of all eligible voters between eighteen and twenty-nine voted in 2008 and 2012, with Obama winning most of their votes, according to Politico. This was a significant leap compared to the 1990s and early 2000s, when only about 40 percent of eligible young people voted.

Barack Obama's presidential campaign helped many people to stop seeing politics as a distant process that didn't involve them, but rather, as an exciting part of community life and something in which they could actively participate.

GETTING TO KNOW THE COMMUNITY

To be effective politicians, candidates need to prove they understand key community problems and present detailed plans to address those problems. Candidates identify community problems in a number of ways. To begin with, they're usually familiar with some

BETO O'ROURKE AND COMMUNITY ORGANIZING

In June 2018, US congressmember Beto O'Rourke, a Democrat from the Texas border town of El Paso, led hundreds of people in a march on the West Texas town of Tornillo, where about two hundred children had been detained after being separated from their parents when attempting to immigrate to or seek asylum in the United States. O'Rourke and his followers were protesting President Donald Trump's policy of separating children from their parents as a measure to prevent undocumented immigrants from entering the country.

At the time, O'Rourke was running for US Senate in a historically Republican state. He knew he needed some Republican voters to switch sides in order to win. Despite knowing the march could hurt his chances with those voters, O'Rourke rallied communities and marched anyway. In doing so, he used a tactic that many candidates fear: taking a very public and firm stance on a controversial issue—in this case, immigration policy. He used his campaign to draw attention to the issue and inspire action. It worked: in the months that followed, busloads of people descended on border towns to protest family separation. O'Rourke, who lost to

Beto O'Rourke used his 2018 Senate campaign to draw attention to controversial problems, like immigration enforcement, that need comprehensive and long-lasting solutions.

(CONTINUED ON THE NEXT PAGE)

(CONTINUED FROM THE PREVIOUS PAGE)

Republican senator Ted Cruz by only three points, sacrificed potential votes to urge communities to act on an important issue.

O'Rourke's Senate campaign drew many comparisons to Obama's youthful, community-centric style. He made an unprecedented effort to meet the people of all 254 Texas counties and unify them over key issues in one of the most intense Senate races in American history. Also, like Obama, many of O'Rourke's supporters were young people from diverse backgrounds who found his energy, passion, and commitment to change inspirational. And while he may have lost his Senate race, O'Rourke's campaign helped him to go from being a little-known congressmember to a national political superstar.

community problems because they are themselves part of the community. When Republican Angel Rivera, a longtime Indianapolis resident, ran for Indianapolis City-County Council in 2010, it was because he'd observed firsthand some critical issues that the city needed to address. "Crime and decaying infrastructure were at the top of my mind. Indianapolis was also getting distracted with less urgent issues," Rivera said in an interview with the author. "But the city could barely balance its budget and had great legacy costs that it faced in the future."

While campaigning, Rivera had to learn about other problems voters cared about, which were often different from the problems that had inspired him to run in the first place. He needed to prove he understood those problems and had plans to address them in addition to his key issues of crime and infrastructure. To do this, he hit the campaign trail and met people from the city's many communities. He then created specific campaign messaging to appeal to various voter communities, all of which cared about issues specific to their communities or had their own unique perspectives on citywide issues. Because he was running for an "at-large" council seat (meaning he'd represent all residents rather than residents within a specific district), Rivera had to appeal to basically everyone. "The urgency of certain issues changed from one group to the next." Rivera's campaign was successful and he was voted into office, where he served as city-county councilor from March 2010 to December 2011.

IDENTIFYING COMMUNITY PROBLEMS

Rivera's campaign is an example of an issues-driven campaign. In an issues-driven campaign, candidates recognize there may be community problems they're not very familiar with because they don't experience them personally. For example, a candidate from an upper middle class neighborhood might not have firsthand experience with the homeless problem in his or her town, but this person will still be responsible for addressing it if elected.

An issues-driven candidate does the legwork to identify as many community problems as possible while also getting to know the people in the district. Candidates might attend local civic meetings or meet with parents and teachers to learn about budget, safety, and educational issues. They may attend various religious services or events sponsored by diverse

Identifying and Documenting a Community Problem for a Political Campaign

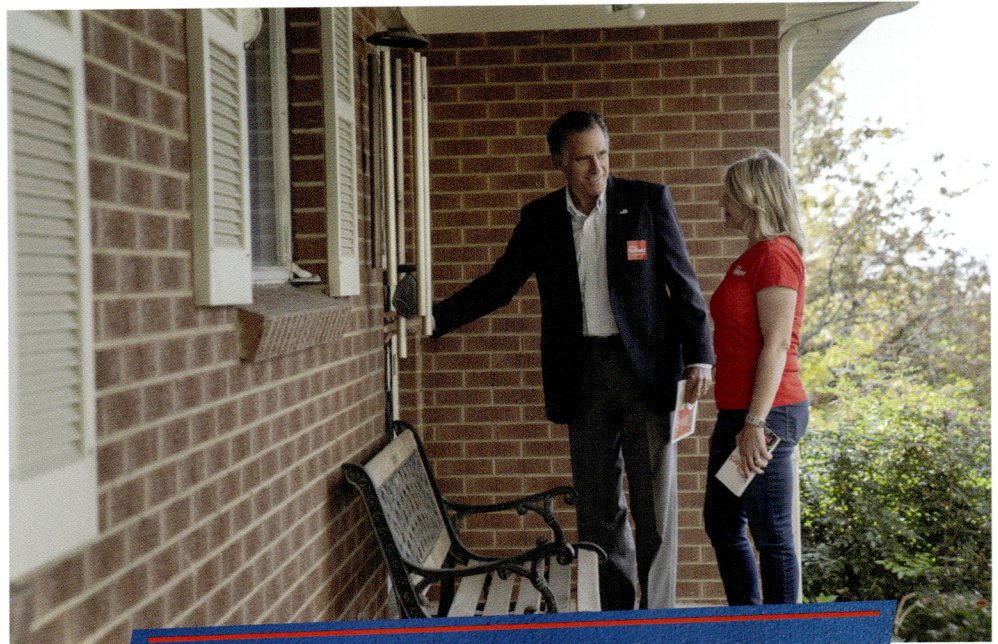

Good political candidates get to know community members and their concerns. They visit different neighborhoods, attend events, and start working on solutions to the problems they learn about.

ethnic groups to learn about the specific concerns of those communities. They might attend public events, where they can meet a lot of different people at once. Some candidates also use old-fashioned, yet effective, campaigning techniques such as knocking on doors or calling people to introduce themselves, share their ideas to address key issues, and learn more about what matters to the people they're talking to.

Through all these methods and more, candidates should develop a strong sense of the problems facing their communities and the steps voters want to see taken to address those problems. Candidates who take an issues-driven approach to campaigning often

Understanding the Community

follow an important campaign tenet: listening more than talking. A good candidate will remember that the campaign is about the voter, not the candidate.

Candidates who fail to do this work usually make poor elected representatives. That's because elected officials are supposed to work on behalf of the people and the issues people care about, and they can't do that if they haven't made the effort to get to know the people they represent.

DOCUMENTING COMMUNITY PROBLEMS

While candidates are identifying community problems before and during their campaigns, they have to take an extra step: documenting what they learn. Well-funded or high-profile campaigns will usually have staff dedicated to researching problems, polling (surveying) the public to find out what matters to people, and compiling the data for the candidate's use in speeches, position statements, and debates. In smaller campaigns, the candidates themselves and their campaign teams will do this research and documentation through meeting or talking directly with members of the public. Most candidates will focus on a handful of community problems to address in their campaigns. Ideally, they'll get to know these problems very well and craft detailed plans to address them. They can use their research to show voters that these problems matter and require the action of dedicated elected representatives. Often, candidates will use their research and data to post position statements

Identifying and Documenting a Community Problem for a Political Campaign

Campaign literature is one way that candidates can document a problem and share their plans to address it. This can help raise awareness of problems and rally voters' support.

on their campaign websites, in press releases, and on campaign literature such as flyers. Candidates are increasingly using the internet to document community problems via social media posts in which they share statistics on problems and their ideas to solve them.

DEVELOPING A POLICY AGENDA

To develop a policy agenda, the Parkland students who formed March for Our Lives combined the evidence that someone like Cruz was capable of violence with the reality that, despite this evidence, he was still able to obtain guns. The organization laid out its policy agenda demanding additional legislation that could prevent the kind of gun violence its founders suffered.

Just like March for Our Lives, political candidates must develop policy agendas. These agendas are usually dictated by the problems that the candidates have identified and documented. The agendas of worthy candidates will show that they put the needs of their communities first by developing and proposing solid solutions to community problems.

CHAPTER THREE

ASSESSING A CANDIDATE

People run for elected office for many reasons. Some see political office as a stepping-stone or résumé builder for their careers. Some run for office because they come from a family of public servants. Some run for office to try to keep their political party in power. Almost all candidates, however, claim a desire to effect meaningful change and address issues as the inspiration to run for office. During campaigns, candidates focus on key issues—a handful of problems and proposed solutions to those problems that define their political agendas. Often, these issues will be a mix of issues that candidates know voters care about and issues the candidates themselves are passionate about. Together, these issues are the legs that hold up a candidate's campaign platform—an official set of goals designed to appeal to voters.

It's not enough for candidates to simply learn about, acknowledge, and document key issues, though. They also need to do the hard work of finding solutions for community problems. Their proposals for addressing key issues are the foundation of their campaigns, but how good are those proposals? How do you know if candidates will follow through on their proposals once elected? Do they genuinely care about the issue or are they just trying to get votes? Do they seem like they'll listen to constituents? Will they be open to working with members of the other party?

There are a number of ways to evaluate political candidates to assess their worthiness. It's crucial to pay attention to how well local or state elected officials represent the people who elected them.

Candidates focus on specific key issues that provide the foundation for their campaign platforms. These issues are generally problems in the community that need to be addressed by elected officials.

Otherwise, ineffectual or morally compromised leaders may continue to be elected to office. So how do you evaluate an elected official's performance?

EVALUATING YOUR REPRESENTATIVES

To start with, review elected officials' voting records alongside a list of their campaign donors. (You can get this information from websites such as votesmart.org and fec.gov. This information will also be useful when assessing incumbent candidates—candidates running for reelection.) If they seem to vote based on donors, political action committees (PACs), or special interest groups (which use money or power to pressure elected representatives to vote in certain ways), they're not voting on your behalf; they're voting to please the people who likely bankroll their reelection campaigns or offer other perks.

In 2018, March for Our Lives took a stand against the influence special interests groups have on politics after the group was repeatedly asked to endorse or support candidates running in the midterm elections. David Hogg, one of the group's founders, posted a powerful reminder for candidates and elected officials: "Don't call us asking for endorsements. The only thing we endorse is common sense policies. Don't call us asking for political donations. If you need money from special interest groups then you shouldn't be running. Sincerely, March For Our Lives."

Another way to assess elected officials is by looking for evidence of "party line" politics, wherein an elected official's legislative priorities and voting patterns are dictated by their political party affiliation (such as Republican or Democrat) rather than by what their constituents want. Because many elected offices don't have term limits, elected officials are often more focused on reelection than they are on legislation. Therefore, they seldom try to appeal to voters from outside their party, openly support the opinions of the opposite political party, or work with the opposing party because their reelection depends on keeping the support of their voting base and political party.

As a result, many members of the two major political parties have become uncompromising in their stances on key issues because their reelection depends on upholding their party's views. If elected officials consistently vote along party lines, they're probably

Good candidates and elected officials put aside party politics to propose or vote on legislation the way most of their constituents want them to—not the way their party dictates.

not putting in the hard work to find out what all their constituents want, regardless of party affiliation. They may even be unwilling to assess the merits of the opposing party's ideas or to pay attention to their own constituents' correspondence about upcoming legislative decisions because they've already decided to vote along party lines before the legislation even goes to a vote.

It is also possible to evaluate elected officials based on their voting records. If they're ineffectual legislators (meaning they write, sponsor, or involve themselves in few legislative bills), then they're not making the most of their ability to work on behalf of their constituents. If an elected official's legislative and voting records show an unwillingness to collaborate or compromise with elected officials from the opposite political party, they may not be doing a good job. Representatives' voting records should reflect whether they've reached across the aisle to work on legislation.

EVALUATING A CANDIDATE DURING A CAMPAIGN

Evaluating candidates and campaigns can be harder than evaluating elected officials. Unlike elected officials, who can be assessed through concrete evidence such as voting and donor records, candidates, especially first timers, can sweep voters off their feet with big promises, charisma, and slogans but may not have any concrete evidence to support these promises. These surface-level characteristics tend to dominate campaign materials, manipulate public perception, attract attention to the candidate rather than the issues, and allow candidates to

Assessing a Candidate

avoid directly addressing anything that might lose them votes (such as taking a stand on controversial issues).

Campaigns can suddenly seem a lot more interesting when you consider whether candidates in your town or state are trying to pull a fast one on voters by using surface-level tactics. If you discern that a candidate is becoming popular by superficial means, it's kind of like finding out that a classmate might get into an Ivy League university by lying about his or her grade point average. When you consider that an undeserving candidate might actually get elected and affect your future, it makes sense that you would want to invest some time and energy to make sure you are

Those who are not old enough to vote can still make their voices heard by participating in community work or attending rallies for issues they care about.

voting for candidates because of their substance rather than their style.

CONSIDER THE ISSUES

What do you care about? The environment? Animals who need homes? Poverty? Money for college? What do you think an elected official should do about the things you care about? These are the first steps in deciding what you want in a candidate who might one day have the power to make laws that affect you and the things you care about. Knowing what issues you care about can also help you figure out which political party you identify with. Or perhaps you see yourself as an independent, someone who sees some good ideas on both sides. Envision what qualities your ideal leaders would have. Do you want them to be smart, sincere, passionate, or have a background in one of the issues you care about (such as environmental activism or helping the homeless)?

LEARN ABOUT THE CANDIDATES

Once you know what issues you care about and the leadership qualities you want in an elected official, consider those issues in the context of a campaign. Chances are, there is an election in the pipeline that you can study. Find out which candidates are running. A good resource for this is VOTE411.org, run by the nonpartisan group League of Women Voters (LWV).

Campaign adviser Gareth Morgans shared some easy places to start learning about candidates:

Assessing a Candidate 35

Every candidate running for office has a campaign website where they list the issues that concern them and why they're running. Visit each website, print out and review the issues, and make a list of questions that you think about as you study their agenda. Reach out to the campaign office, or better yet, attend a candidate forum and ask your questions directly to the candidate.

As you go, collect campaign literature, mailers, press reports, advertising, video or transcripts of campaign

Get to know the people running for office. Find out when candidates are holding forums or events near you so you can meet them, ask questions, and share your ideas.

speeches, and information about candidates' debates (which may be covered by the media or campaign headquarters may have video records). Once you've collected these materials, review them to find out where the candidates stand on issues you care about. Morgans had the following advice for this step:

> Always make sure to review and cross reference any facts the candidate may use, and always ensure the source material is from a legitimate organization. One of the best resources is your local (credible) newspaper or TV stations: have they screened the candidate and what questions did they ask? How did the candidates respond?
>
> The League of Women Voters (LWV) is also a good resource for information about candidates in local, state, and federal races.

ASSESS WHETHER THEY WILL BE GOOD LEADERS

Knowing whether candidates will make good elected officials is difficult. Both first-time and incumbent candidates can use campaigns to convince voters that things will be different if they're elected. How do you truly vet the leadership abilities of the people behind the campaign glitz?

First, investigate candidates' experience. Do they have professional backgrounds, advocacy experience, or a history of community involvement that has prepared them for the challenges of elected office?

BEWARE OF DISTORTION TECHNIQUES

All candidates are vying for public support. Many rely on traits that make them popular, like good public speaking skills or personal charisma, to create the appearance of worthiness rather than really addressing the issues. How can you see through this? Look for "distortion techniques" that campaigns employ to manipulate voters. Here's a list of common distortion techniques from the LWV:

- Name-calling or prejudicial attacks based on opponents' characteristics that have nothing to do with political ability, such as race or religion
- Starting or spreading rumors about an opponent without evidence of wrongdoing; just implying the opponent may be guilty of something is often damaging enough
- Guilt by association, wherein a candidate attacks an opponent based on the opponent's supporters, such as endorsements from advocacy groups or donors
- Catchwords used to elicit emotional responses instead of inform voters (such as "un-American")
- Blaming an opponent for something he or she couldn't control in order to cover up the candidate's own responsibility
- Making unrealistic promises
- Evasiveness, such as avoiding answering questions about issues, giving ambiguous responses, or mentioning the benefits of a solution without giving specifics about how to carry out the solution

Beyond that list, look for evidence that candidates are staging public appearances to get attention from the press, such as rallies filled with patriotic paraphernalia and supporters clad in campaign shirts and buttons. Are candidates using these appearances to shout about what's wrong in the community or attack an opponent without offering their own specific ideas to solve problems? Also, keep an eye on campaign ads (especially on television or online) in which candidates viciously attack an opponent or appeal to people's patriotism and emotions instead of discussing their own qualifications and ideas. By identifying these manipulative campaign techniques, you can identify whether candidates are blowing smoke or if they're for real.

Take a hard look at their campaign activities using this advice from the LWV: "Do they give speeches to different groups—even those groups that may disagree with the candidates' views on issues? Do they accept invitations to debate? Do the campaigns emphasize media events, where the candidates can be seen but not heard?" (An example of a "seen but not heard" event is a candidate cutting a ribbon to open a new bridge rather than talking about real transportation issues facing the community. This type of appearance gives the impression of leadership and community involvement but it doesn't actually require candidates to prove they can address key issues.)

FIND OUT WHAT OTHERS THINK

Find out what other people in your community think of the candidates running in upcoming elections. Ask family members and community members (such as business owners or local volunteers) whom they support and why. Get a list of candidates' endorsements from interest groups or organizations. Learn what those groups represent and consider why they endorsed the candidate—is it because they believe the candidate will do good work to address community problems or because they hope the candidate will represent their interests once elected?

Find out who's donated to candidates' campaigns (a good source for this is the website www.opensecrets.org). How will these donations affect how candidates behave as elected officials? Will they

Assessing a Candidate   39

Figuring out whether a candidate deserves your support can be hard. To get perspective, ask people in your life and in the community what they think about the candidates.

feel compelled to, for instance, recommend a certain company for a government contract because someone from that company donated to their campaign?

What others think about a candidate can help you put your own thoughts and opinions into perspective. However, don't let their opinions undermine your own. You've done your research and thought about the candidates in terms of the things you care about. Use your instincts and your evidence as launchpads into political and community involvement.

CHAPTER FOUR

IT'S YOUR TURN

However far away a problem like gun violence or climate change may seem from your personal experience, the causes of most problems are likely present in your community. For example, you may know people who struggle with emotional or developmental issues that, if untreated, may lead them to commit violence. Perhaps someone in your life has behaved in a way that you found concerning or offensive. Maybe your town doesn't recycle or make an effort to educate the public about environmental conservation. Perhaps the local animal shelter euthanizes far more animals than it gets adopted. All these scenarios present a chance for you to become involved in solving problems in your community.

Gareth Morgans has this advice:

Find something that you're passionate about and begin researching the issue. Find legitimate research to back up your passion and start researching who, within your community, is

What problems in your community do you care about? You don't have to be old enough to vote to do something about them. You can start making a difference now.

passionate about the same issue and how they are advocating for it. Are they working with their city council member or county commissioner? Maybe it's a state or federal issue and they're working with their state senator or member of Congress. Every voice counts during a discussion, and making sure your voice is heard is vital to both democracy and creating long-term, effective policy change.

WORKING WITHIN YOUR COMMUNITY

Overcoming the limitations of elected offices, confusion over how different levels of government work, and the pitfalls of party politics depends a great deal on people setting aside differences to work toward solutions. In her book *Smart Communities: How Citizens and Local Leaders Can Use Strategic Thinking to Build a Brighter Future*, Suzanne W. Morse says, "Democracy becomes real for people when they move beyond the political candidate or campaign they support and decide what kind of community they want."

Politics has become adversarial, with status quo leadership losing sight of what's best for everyone. This is where community comes in. As evidenced by Barack Obama's early days in Chicago, solutions don't have to come from the government alone. Communities and the people in them can make change happen, and, in the process, develop leaders and potential elected officials who understand everyday challenges. As Morse writes, "Communities need leaders who come through the ranks and from the rank and file … Leadership occurs when individuals step up to the plate on important issues and when they are prepared to take on the difficult work."

START LOCALLY

The students responsible for March for Our Lives don't just hold public rallies and chant about putting an end to gun violence. They have identified problems (gun violence and lax regulations regarding purchasing firearms), researched the specific issues underlying those problems, and continued to lobby the state and federal governments to address those issues. March for Our Lives may have grown into a national organization by identifying school shootings and gun violence as national issues, but it started as a response to a local issue: the school shooting in Parkland, Florida.

"All politics is local," says Morgan. He advises students to find neighborhood civic clubs, where they can get involved on a grassroots level and discuss

Young people, like those who started March for Our Lives, can identify, research, and brainstorm solutions to community problems. Elected officials should listen to what they have to say.

concerns with neighbors, community members, and civic club leaders. Those leaders often have direct contact with elected officials. Involvement in a local civic organization could provide you with a path directly to an elected representative who could do something about an issue you care about.

SPEAK UP

It's important for local government bodies, like city councils and school boards, to know the people they serve. The concerns and desires of the people in your community should dictate what those local governments do. Young people can get involved by visiting city hall to meet the mayor and city council members. They can sit in on a school board meeting. The town's and school district's websites should have information about the people elected to sit on these governing bodies as well as the agendas for upcoming meetings. These agendas can give you valuable information about what issues are up for a vote at upcoming meetings.

Your local representatives may be discussing or voting on an issue you care about at a future meeting. If not, you can attend their meetings and write them letters to voice your opinions and ask them to do something about an issue you care about. To make your arguments strong, pin down a community problem you care about (like the animals at the local shelter or your curriculum at school) and gather evidence about the issue. (For example, find out how many animals currently need adoption or compare your school's curriculum to that of other school districts.) Document the opinions of other people who share your concerns. Develop your opinion about what should change based on the evidence and what others think. Visualize the solution and use your documentation to back that solution up when you speak at a local government meeting or write a letter to your local elected officials.

A lot of communities have groups of people who are already active in trying to solve problems. Through the local animal shelter, for example, you may be able to find information about nonprofit groups dedicated to helping animals find homes. Ask someone at city hall about local groups that work to help the homeless, protect the environment, or work on other causes

By identifying problems in your community, you can likely find existing organizations that are addressing those problems. These organizations may appreciate your help.

you want to champion. These groups usually need all the help they can get from volunteers who can provide hands-on assistance, get the word out, help gather supplies, and add their voices to the call for change. The parent-teacher association might already be fighting for curriculum changes; these groups usually welcome input from students. Through your participation with existing groups that care about what you care about, your call to action can be even louder, increasing the chance that you'll be heard by elected officials—and get the attention of candidates looking for key issues to define their campaigns.

CAMPAIGNS IN YOUR COMMUNITY

In May 2017, eighteen-year-old Mikael "Mike" Floyd, a high school student in the Houston suburb of Pearland, Texas, defeated a two-term incumbent candidate in his school district's Board of Trustees election by winning 54 percent of the vote. In addition to his young age, Floyd faced other challenges, such as his opponent receiving high-profile endorsements and having actual experience on the Board of Trustees. "We were the underdog in every way imaginable," Floyd told the local CBS station, KHOU. Despite these challenges, Floyd became one of the youngest elected officials in the country. "Floyd attributed his election success to having firsthand experience as a student in the district (he was a senior at the time of his election), campaigning on the issues affecting families in the school district, a growing desire for anti-establishment candidates, and the

IT TAKES A VILLAGE

Former secretary of state and presidential nominee Hillary Clinton once wrote a book called *It Takes a Village*. In it, she put forward the view that raising children is a societal responsibility, and that many institutions—like family, extended family, neighbors, schools, faith communities, medical professionals, and social and governmental groups—are all responsible for ensuring that children get the attention and care they need to be successful and happy.

Every community, regardless of size, location, or demographics, has people who need help. In some communities, these people get the help they need. In others, there may be underlying problems preventing people in need from getting the help they need. These problems may include insufficient funding for schools, too few professionals available or willing to intervene in a troubled person's life, and too few proactive community members willing to step up to help someone who is alone and in trouble.

While Clinton's "it takes a village" philosophy was controversial—critics said individuals should be responsible for their own behavior rather than communities stepping in to help raise children—most people can probably agree that it's better to address community problems before they result in a tragedy. Identifying those problems, studying them, and actively addressing them are all actions young people can take to make their own communities better. What's more, young people can help governmental bodies, like school boards, city councils, state legislatures, and even Congress, better understand the problems their communities face.

desire for systemic change," Morgans, Houston-based political consultant, said.

Not every young person who wants to help make change happen has to run for local office, as Floyd did. You can start close to home with involvement in

Many political campaigns rely on young people to get involved in all kinds of ways. Use your strengths and interests to find a candidate you'd like to help get elected.

civic clubs, as Morgans suggests, but you can also get involved by working with political campaigns. That's how Angel Rivera, the former Indianapolis City-County councilor, got his start. "There are many opportunities at the local level, including nonprofits and appointed boards, that can introduce a young person to public service," Rivera said. "I began by getting involved in campaigns and later in public boards. With effort, you can quickly become a change agent in your own community."

JOIN A CAMPAIGN

Campaigns are a great way to tackle an issue you care about while also helping a candidate who shares your concerns and vision for the future. Morgans said:

> Find an issue you're passionate about and find a candidate that supports that issue or has advocated for that issue in the past. Get involved with a candidate's campaign. Political campaigns are always looking for student organizers, volunteers, and Get Out the Vote (GOTV) squads. Find a candidate that you feel best shares your principles and contact their campaign. Ask to speak to a field organizer and explain why you're supporting the candidate and what skills you have that you feel would benefit the campaign.

If your research on candidates running for local, state, or federal office shows that none of those candidates is speaking about an issue you care about, contact the candidates' campaigns and ask them to consider adding your issue to the list of issues they're running on. Candidates may need your help identifying a problem in the community. Use your passion and research to get them to care about it, too.

RAISE YOUR VOICE

Whether through your school's student government, your town council or school board, your state and federal elected officials, or candidates' campaigns, you

Find a way to act on the things you care about. Participate in the political process on some level, whether it's at your school or in the broader community.

have many opportunities to make your voice heard. Don't pass up this chance. Young people can make an immense difference in the lives of many people. Public officials and candidates should take community problems seriously and work toward solving them, and young people can assist in that effort. It just takes a willingness to learn about community problems and the courage to bring those problems to the attention of public officials and candidates running for office. Even if you are not old enough to vote, that doesn't mean you don't have a voice. Speak up and make someone listen!

GLOSSARY

advocacy Support of a particular cause, policy, or group of people.
campaign To work toward the goal of getting elected to a public office.
candidate A person who runs for public office.
community A group of people who live in the same area or who have certain traits or characteristics in common.
community organizing Coordinating the efforts of local residents to further their community's interests.
Congress The two groups of elected officials—the House of Representatives and the Senate—that represent voters in national government.
election A process in which a group of people vote.
electorate The people who are entitled to vote in an election.
legislation Considering and making laws as part of a governing body.
legislature The legislative body of a country or state.
midterm election An election in which voters can elect representatives and other officeholders (such as state representatives or members of a local council) in the middle of the executive officer's term.
nonpartisan Not biased toward any particular political party, cause, or person.
party line A political party or group's official opinion, policy, or agenda.
platform The stated policy or policies of a political party, group, or candidate.
policy A course of action or principle proposed by or adopted by a government, party, or individual.

political party A group of people who work together because they share similar ideas.

representative A person chosen or elected to speak and act on behalf of others.

republic A country or state in which the power is held by the people and their elected representatives and which has an elected or nominated president.

term limits Restrictions on the number of times an elected representative can run for and hold a particular public office.

voter A person who has the right to cast a vote in an election.

voting base A group of voters who typically always support a single party's candidates for elected office.

FOR MORE INFORMATION

Canadian Alliance of Student Associations (CASA)
130 Slater Street, Suite 410
Ottawa, ON, K1P 6E2
Canada
Website: http://www.casa-acae.com
Facebook, Instagram, and Twitter: @CASAACAE
CASA is a nonpartisan nonprofit student organization composed of multiple student associations from across Canada. The organization advocates for students, and Canada's leaders consult with CASA on decisions affecting the education system.

Inspire Democracy
30 Victoria Street
Gatineau, QC K1A 0M6
Canada
(800) 463-6868
Website: http://www.inspirerlademocratie -inspiredemocracy.ca
Facebook: @ElectionsCanE
Twitter: @ElectionsCan_E
Inspire Democracy, an initiative of Elections Canada, aims to encourage youth civic engagement. The organization provides information on everything from voter turnout and voter registration data to civic participation and how political parties engage with youth.

Millennial Action Project (MAP)
1875 Connecticut Avenue NW, 10th Floor
Washington, DC 20009

(202) 480-2051
Website: http://www.millennialaction.org
Facebook: @MillennialActionProject
Twitter: @MActionProject
MAP is the largest nonpartisan organization of millennial policymakers in the United States. The organization works to overcome partisanship through future-focused challenges and democracy reforms.

National Democratic Institute (NDI)
455 Massachusetts Avenue NW, 8th Floor
Washington, DC 20001
(202) 728-5500
Website: http://www.ndi.org
Facebook: @National.Democratic.Institute
Instagram: @ndidemocracy
Twitter: @NDI
NDI is a nonprofit nonpartisan organization that supports democratic institutions and practices all over the world. NDI promotes openness and accountability in government by building political and civic organizations, safeguarding elections, and promoting citizen participation.

Reboot Democracy
Website: http://www.rebootdem.com
Facebook, Instagram, and Twitter: @RebootDem
This nonprofit creates a comprehensive ecosystem of support for early-stage innovators who are building technology to strengthen democracy. The organization helps other innovative groups and

individuals, especially women and minorities, to connect and collaborate.

She Should Run
80 M Street SE, Floor 1
Washington, DC 20003
(202) 796-8396
Website: http://www.sheshouldrun.org
Facebook, Instagram, and Twitter: @sheshouldrun
She Should Run provides community, resources, and growth opportunities for women who are interested in running for public office.

Youth Service America (YSA)
1050 Connecticut Avenue NW, Room 65525
Washington, DC 20035
(202) 296-2992
Website: http://www.ysa.org or http://leadasap.ysa.org
Facebook: @youthserviceamerica
Twitter: @youthservice
YSA supports a global culture of engaged children and youth committed to a lifetime of meaningful service, learning, and leadership. The YSA websites feature the stories of young people who make a difference in their communities, encouraging newcomers to make a difference on their own.

FOR FURTHER READING

Cunningham, Kevin. *How Political Campaigns and Elections Work*. Minneapolis, MN: Core Library, 2015.

Fleischer, Jeff. *Votes of Confidence: A Young Person's Guide to American Elections*. San Francisco, CA: Zest Books, 2016.

Gunderson, Jessica. *Understanding Your Role in Elections*. North Mankato, MN: Capstone Press, 2018.

Harper, Leslie. *How to Contact an Elected Official*. New York, NY: Rosen Publishing, 2015.

Houser, Grace. *Understanding US Elections and the Electoral College*. New York, NY: Rosen Publishing, 2018.

Jacobs, Natalie, and Thomas A. Jacobs. *Every Vote Matters: The Power of Your Voice, From Student Elections to the Supreme Court*. Minneapolis, MN: Free Spirit Publishing, 2016.

Klepeis, Alicia Z. *Understanding the Electoral College*. New York, NY: Rosen Publishing, 2018.

Loria, Laura. *What Is the Constitution?* New York, NY: Rosen Publishing, 2016.

Machajewski, Sarah. *What Are State and Local Governments*? New York, NY: Rosen Publishing, 2016.

Martin, Bobi. *What Are Elections?* New York, NY: Rosen Publishing, 2016.

Small, Cathleen. *Elections and Voting*. New York, NY: Lucent Press, 2019.

Weiss, Nancy E. *Asking Questions About Political Campaigns*. Ann Arbor, MI: Cherry Lake Publishing, 2016.

BIBLIOGRAPHY

Aguilar, Julián. "Beto O'Rourke and Other Democrats Urge Public to Keep Tornillo Migrant Facility in Spotlight." *Texas Tribune*, December 15, 2018. https://www.texastribune.org/2018/12/15/beto-orourke-democrats-tornillo.

Aguilar, Julián, and Juan Luis García Hernández. "Beto O'Rourke, Veronica Escobar lead Father's Day March on Tent City Housing Separated Immigrant Children." *Texas Tribune*, June 17, 2018. https://www.texastribune.org/2018/06/17/texas-beto-orourke-tent-city-tornillo-immigration.

Berkowitz, Bill. "Section 5. Analyzing Community Problems." Community Tool Box, Center for Community Health and Development at the University of Kansas. Retrieved January 29, 2019. https://ctb.ku.edu/en/table-of-contents/assessment/assessing-community-needs-and-resources/analyzing-community-problems/main.

Berman, Mark, et al. "Florida Shooting Suspect Nikolas Cruz: Guns, Depression and a Life in Trouble." *Washington Post*, February 15, 2018. https://www.washingtonpost.com/news/morning-mix/wp/2018/02/15/florida-shooting-suspect-nikolas-cruz-guns-depression-and-a-life-in-free-fall/?utm_term=.e71ccb1cd9dd.

Bernstein, Jackie. "4 Problems in Your Community That Need Your Attention & How You Can Help." Bustle, November 3, 2015. https://www.bustle.com/articles/118926-4-problems-in-your-community-that-need-your-attention-how-you-can-help.

Bump, Philip. "Eighteen Years of Gun Violence in US Schools, Mapped." *Washington Post*, February 14, 2018. https://www.washingtonpost.com/news/politics/wp/2018/02/14/eighteen-years-of-gun-violence-in-u-s-schools-mapped/?noredirect=on&utm_term=.7d41f25864ee.

Bump, Philip. "4.4 million 2012 Obama Voters Stayed Home in 2016 — More Than a Third of Them Black." *Washington Post*, March 12, 2018. https://www.washingtonpost.com/news/politics/wp/2018/03/12/4-4-million-2012-obama-voters-stayed-home-in-2016-more-than-a-third-of-them-black/?noredirect=on&utm_term=.8f57e8f6e2d3.

Chuck, Elizabeth, Alex Johnson, and Corky Siemaszko. "17 Killed in Mass Shooting at High School in Parkland, Florida." NBC News, February 14, 2018. https://www.nbcnews.com/news/us-news/police-respond-shooting-parkland-florida-high-school-n848101.

Hogg, David (@davidhogg111). "Dear Politicians, Don't call us asking for endorsements. The only thing we endorse is common sense policies. Don't call us asking for political donations. If you need money from special interest groups then you shouldn't be running. Sincerely, March For Our Lives." Twitter, July 12, 2018. https://twitter.com/davidhogg111/status/1017528364507131904.

Kovaleski, Serge. "Obama's Organizing Years, Guiding Others and Finding Himself." *New York Times*, July 7, 2008. http://www.nytimes.com/2008/07/07/us/politics/07community.html.

Bibliography

League of Women Voters. "How to Judge a Candidate." August 19, 2008. https://www.lwv.org/educating-voters/how-judge-candidate.

Marcotte, Amanda. "Hillary Clinton Defies Right-Wing Critics, Endorses Universal Pre-K." Slate, June 18, 2015. https://slate.com/human-interest/2015/06/conservatives-hate-it-takes-a-village-hillary-clinton-embraces-it-by-endorsing-universal-pre-k.html.

Mazzei, Patricia. "Parkland Shooting Suspect Lost Special-Needs Help at School When He Needed It Most." *New York Times*, April 4, 2018. https://www.nytimes.com/2018/08/04/us/parkland-florida-nikolas-cruz.html.

McLaughlin, Eliot C., and Madison Park. "School Shooter's Past Includes Buying Guns, Cutting, Slurs and Mental Illness." CNN, February 20, 2018. http://www.cnn.com/2018/02/19/us/florida-school-shooting/index.html.

Meyer, Cheryl Diaz, Becky Harlan, and Eric Lee. "Students Make Their Stand at DC's 'March For Our Lives.'" National Public Radio, March 25, 2018. https://www.npr.org/2018/03/25/596760836/photos-students-make-their-stand-at-d-c-s-march-for-our-lives.

Morgans, Gareth (political consultant). In discussion with the author, Houston, Texas, March 6, 2019.

Morse, Suzanne W. *Smart Communities: How Citizens and Local Leaders Can Use Strategic Thinking to Build a Brighter Future*. San Francisco, CA: Jossey-Bass, 2014.

National Democratic Institute. "Campaign Skills Trainer's Guide: Identifying Issues and Developing Policy Positions." Retrieved January 25, 2019. https://www.ndi.org.

Rivera, Angel (former Indianapolis City-County Councillor). In discussion with the author, Irving, Texas, February 6, 2019.

Robillard, Kevin. "Study: Youth Vote Was Decisive." Politico, November 7, 2012. https://www.politico.com/story/2012/11/study-youth-vote-was-decisive-083510.

Schwartzman, Edward. *Political Campaign Craftsmanship: A Professional's Guide to Campaigning for Public Office.* New York, NY: Routledge, 2017.

Smith, Brandi. "Pearland Student, 18, Beats Incumbent for School Board Seat." KHOU, May 7, 2017. https://www.khou.com/article/news/local/pearland-student-18-beats-incumbent-for-school-board-seat/285-437624238.

INDEX

A

addiction, 13
advocacy
  experience with, 36
  groups, 37
  for an issue, 40–41, 49
animal shelter, 40, 44, 45

B

budget, 22, 23

C

candidates
  assessing, 36, 38
  demands of, 6, 15
  incumbent, 30, 36, 46
  learning about issues, 23, 25
  successful, 19, 20
  voters learning about, 9
  winning over constituents, 9, 11–12, 24–25
city council, 10, 41, 44, 47
civic clubs, 43–44, 47–48
Clinton, Hillary, 47
community organizers, 17, 20
community organizing
  and Beto O'Rourke, 21–22
  as great education, 18–19
Congress, 10, 41, 47
congressional district, 7
congressmember, 21, 22
crime, 22
Cruz, Nikolas, 4, 13, 14, 26–27
Cruz, Ted, 21–22

D

democracy, 8, 20, 41, 42
Democrats, 6, 19, 20, 21, 30–31
Developing Communities Project (DCP), 17, 18–19
discrimination, 13
distortion techniques, 37
donations, 30, 38

E

elected officials, 5, 6, 7, 10, 25, 29, 30–32, 34, 36, 38, 42, 44, 45, 46–47, 49–50
Election Day, 12
elections
  midterm, 6, 11, 30
  and money, 30
  of Obama, 18–19, 20
  point of, 15, 16, 23, 25, 28, 29, 30, 31, 33–34, 36
  researching, 38
  what's interesting about, 8–9
  yearly, 11
electorate, 19
endorsements, 30, 37, 38, 46
environment, 9, 13, 34, 40, 45–46

F

Floyd, Mikael "Mike," 46, 47

G

gun control
  laws, 4–5, 6
  problem of, 13–14, 26–27, 42–43

H

health care, 9, 13
homelessness, 13, 23, 34, 45–46
House of Representatives, 6, 10

I

inequality, 13
infrastructure, 22
issues, 6, 8, 9, 11, 12, 13, 21–22, 23, 24, 28–29, 31, 32–33, 34, 35, 36, 37, 38, 40–41, 42–43, 44, 46–47, 49
  gun control, 6
  taxation, 10
issues-driven campaigns, 24–25

L

League of Women Voters (LWV), 34, 36, 37, 38
legislation
  guided by party, 30–31, 32
  gun control, 5, 6, 27
  reactive nature of, 15
literature, campaign, 11, 25–26, 35–36

M

March for Our Lives, 5, 6, 14, 26–27, 30, 42, 43
Marjory Stoneman Douglas High School, shooting at, 4, 13
  survivors of, 5, 6
mayor, 10, 11, 44
midterm elections, 6, 11, 30
Morgans, Gareth, 16, 34–35, 36, 40, 46–48, 49
Morse, Suzanne W., 42

O

Obama, Barack, 17, 20
  as community organizer, 18–19
  early days of, 17, 18–19, 42
  political career of, 18–19
  presidential campaign of, 19, 20
  style of, 22
O'Rourke, Beto, 21–22

P

party line politics, 30–31, 32
platform, 28
policy
  change, 41
  child separation, 21

common sense, 30
developing an agenda for, 6, 26–27
immigration, 21
political party, 28, 31, 32, 34
   affiliation, 30–31
poverty, 13, 34
president, 10, 21
   campaign, 17, 19, 20
   election, 20
   nominee, 19, 47
   term of, 11

R

rallies, 11, 19–20, 37, 42
recession, 13
reelection, 30, 31
representatives, 6, 10, 11, 25, 44
   evaluating, 30–32
   voting records of, 32
Rivera, Angel, 22, 23, 48

S

school boards, 10, 11, 44, 46, 47, 49–50
   meetings, 44
school shootings, 4, 5, 13, 14, 43
special interest groups, 30
state legislatures, 10, 47

T

term limits, 31
transportation, 13, 38

V

violence, 13–14, 26–27, 40
   domestic, 13
   gun, 6, 27, 40, 42–43
voters, 6, 9, 10, 11–12, 15, 20, 21, 22, 24, 25, 28, 31, 32, 33, 36, 37
   communities, 23
voting base, 31
voting records, 30, 32

ABOUT THE AUTHOR

Angie Timmons is a writer and communications consultant who has worked on two US congressional campaigns and one state campaign leading up to the 2018 midterm elections. She cochairs the communications committee of a local women's political group and is active in other political and activist organizations. She has written multiple books for Rosen Publishing, including histories of World War II, the Cold War, the Nanjing Massacre, and racism, with a heavy emphasis on the politics behind those subjects. She lives with her husband and their three cats in the Dallas area.

PHOTO CREDITS

Cover Marc Romanelli/Getty Images; pp. 4–5 (background graphics) weerawan/iStock/Getty Images; p. 5 Paul Morigi/Getty Images; p. 8 Joseph Sohm/Shutterstock.com; p. 9 William Thomas Cain/Getty Images; p. 11 Simone Hogan/Shutterstock.com; p. 14 Irina Boriskina/Shutterstock.com; pp. 15, 24, 26 Bloomberg/Getty Images; p. 19 Spencer Platt/Getty Images; p. 21 Paul Ratje/AFP/Getty Images; p. 29 Don Emmert/AFP/Getty Images; pp. 31, 45 Jeffrey Greenberg/UIG/Getty Images; p. 33 Andrew Lichtenstein/Corbis News/Getty Images; p. 35 NurPhoto/Getty Images; p. 39 gawrav/E+/Getty Images; p. 41 Dragon Images/Shutterstock.com; p. 43 Brendan Smialowski/AFP/Getty Images; p. 48 Barbara Davidson/Getty Images; p. 50 Jupiter Images/Photos.com/Getty Images; additional graphic elements moodboard - Mike Watson Images/Brand X Pictures/Getty Images (chapter opener backgrounds), Maksim M/Shutterstock.com (fists).

Design and Layout: Michael Moy; Editor: Rachel Aimee; Photo Researcher: Nicole DiMella